# Dialectics of Secularization

JOSEPH CARDINAL RATZINGER
(Pope Benedict XVI)
and
JÜRGEN HABERMAS

# Dialectics of Secularization

## *On Reason and Religion*

Edited with a Foreword by Florian Schuller

*Translated by Brian McNeil, C.R.V.*

IGNATIUS PRESS    SAN FRANCISCO

Original German edition:
*Dialektik der Säkularisierung: Über Vernunft und Religion*
© 2005 by Herder Verlag, Freiburg im Breisgau

Cover: photograph of Jürgen Habermas and Joseph Ratzinger
by Katholische Akademie in Bayern, München

Cover design by R·M·E München / Roland Eschlbeck

© Libreria Editrice Vaticana
© 2006 by Ignatius Press, San Francisco
ISBN 978-1-58617-166-7
Library of Congress Control Number 2006922749
Printed in the United States of America ∞

# Contents

# *Foreword*

Jürgen Habermas celebrated his seventy-fifth birthday on June 18, 2004, and Joseph Ratzinger was elected Pope on April 19, 2005. These were certainly very different occasions; yet, both times, most of those who praised the two men in the leading German-language newspapers recalled (naturally, from different perspectives) the dialogue between these intellectual "antipodes" in Munich, at the invitation of the Catholic Academy of Bavaria, on January 19, 2004. It is surely no exaggeration to say that this encounter between one of the most important contemporary philosophers and the then Prefect of the Roman Congregation for the Doctrine of the Faith attracted worldwide attention. At that time, we received enquiries here in Munich from as far away as Morocco and Iran.

A few months later, numerous articles marking Habermas' birthday reflected once more on the consequences of that encounter, and even today, the surprise—indeed, sometimes the bewilderment—on the part of his friends and foes has not yet died down. And after the papal election, when the need was felt to present the intellectual and theological profile of Benedict XVI, minds turned almost automatically to that debate about the foundations of our secular Western society which the Cardinal had developed in his reflections on the structure of the worldwide interreligious dialogue.

## Impulses

How did this remarkable evening come about? It had its origin in impressions from outside the German linguistic sphere.

On June 15, 1995, the "Immortals" of the Académie française welcomed into their ranks the Archbishop of Paris, Jean Marie Cardinal Lustiger. He received the fourth seat, in succession to Albert Cardinal Decourtray. Three years earlier, Joseph Cardinal Ratzinger had been elected a "foreign associate member" of the Académie des sciences morales et politiques at the Institut de France.

In recent years, a very intensive, open, and

committed discussion has been going on in Italy between intellectual representatives of the *credenti* ("believers") and the *laici* ("secular persons"), to use the customary abbreviations for these groups with their different world views. One of the most exciting documents to come out of this discussion is certainly the famous number 2/2000 of the left-wing intellectual and political periodical *MicroMega*. The following thesis is formulated in the foreword: "Philosophy is concerned more and more with religion, rather than with knowledge, and seeks to enter a dialogue with religion." This thesis draws for support on philosophical texts from a variety of schools, all of which display a high intellectual quality, and these texts are accompanied by essays by three theologians. The first, which lays bare in a new manner the theological and spiritual drama of German Idealism, is by Bruno Forte (recently appointed Archbishop of Chieti-Vasti), whom I myself regard as the most exciting contemporary Italian theologian. The second essay is by Enzo Bianchi, the founder of the monastery of Bose. The most prominent author is Joseph Cardinal Ratzinger, whom the foreword to the periodical describes as "the quintessence of Catholic orthodoxy".

The editor of *MicroMega* quotes a letter in which the Cardinal writes that he finds it "interesting" that his essay will appear in a periodical that primarily publishes articles by unbelievers—and which has only recently subjected the papal encyclical on philosophy, *Ratio et Fides*, to a harsh critique. Why then is the Cardinal willing to contribute to *MicroMega*? He wishes "to stimulate the debate on the truth of the Christian religion". Precisely this was the subject of the debate in Italy at the turn of the millennium.

If we compare this edition of *MicroMega* with a German publication with a similar theme, such as number 149 of the periodical *Kursbuch* (September 2002), we immediately note the characteristic differences between the two intellectual situations. In the *Kursbuch*, on the theme "God is dead and lives", the situation of the various religions—in the United States or in Israel or in Germany, and including Islam and Hinduism—is described on a consistently high intellectual level. The material is presented by skilled journalists; in part, they are drawing on personal experiences, and yet their perspective is largely one of distance. The review sections of the interregional broadsheet newspapers do indeed debate fundamental philosophical, ethical, and religious questions; but we in Germany seem to lack a common philosophical dialogue on the basis of different positions that are interested in each other (as in Italy) or structures that permit a plurality of world views to engage in a societally institutionalized yet completely free conversation on a high level of reflection (as in France).

One further impulse finally led to the dialogue on January 19, 2004. Three weeks after the terrorist attacks on September 11, 2001, Jürgen Habermas gave his Frankfurt acceptance speech on the occasion of receiving the Peace Prize of the German Booksellers. This address caused a great stir. The philosopher, who describes himself as a follower of Max Weber in the sense that he sees himself as "tone deaf in the religious sphere", surprised many people by demanding that the secular society acquire a new understanding of religious convictions, which are something more and something other than mere relics of a past with which we are finished. On the contrary, these convictions pose a "cognitive challenge" to philosophy. This speech was described by some as "opening a door" for the Churches. It appeared, however, that no one was willing to go through that particular door.

## Academy

There are, of course, already places for discussion that are consciously dedicated to the search for truth and make the contribution of their own convictions—without false modesty, but in a spirit of openness—to the intellectual and reflective exchange of arguments. Traditionally, these places have been the academies. After 1945, the horror born of the experience of terror and war, and the awareness of our responsibility to help in the construction of a society that respected human dignity, led to the foundation of the Church academies in Germany. The Catholic and Protestant Churches were committed to making these academies a success.

During his time as archbishop in Munich, Joseph Cardinal Ratzinger was an enthusiastic Protector of the Catholic Academy of Bavaria, which, since its founding in 1957, has taken up fundamental questions both in public meetings and behind closed doors: questions of ecclesiastical doctrine, of societal reality, of political and economic decisions, and of cultural trends. This is why it seemed obvious that we should try, at least on one occasion, to do something that is taken for granted as a part of the cultural landscape in France or in Italy, namely, to invite these two persons, whose names each stand for a whole intellectual (and cultural) world, to talk to each other.

## (Almost) parallel lives

These two dialogue partners offer the prospect of the most exciting debate imaginable (and not only in the German-language sphere) on basic questions concerning human existence. This makes it all the more surprising that they had in fact never met each other before January 19, 2004, still less sat together on the same podium.

One could speak of almost parallel lives. It is well known that parallel lines meet only at the point of infinity (although I do not intend to insinuate by these words that the Catholic Academy of Bavaria is the point of infinity!). Both dialogue partners belong to the same generation, born in the late 1920s (Ratzinger in 1927, Habermas in 1929). Ratzinger took his doctorate in 1953, Habermas in 1954, each in his own discipline. Both were directly involved—Ratzinger in Tübingen from 1966, Habermas in Frankfurt am Main from 1964—in the initial dramas that were to lead to years of upheaval. Those years saw uncontrolled, often irrational rejections of tradition, and this led both men to a decisive clarification of their convictions. After a number of moves—Ratzinger was Archbishop of Munich and Freising from 1977 to 1981, then Prefect of the Sacred Congregation for the Doctrine of the Faith in Rome; Habermas returned to Frankfurt in 1983 for his final professorial chair, this time for philosophy, with the emphasis on the philosophy of society and of history—both men increasingly made their mark on the ongoing debates in society,

raising their voices in challenge. In the eyes of
the public, the one is the personification of the
Catholic faith, thanks to his understanding of
God, man, and the world; the other is seen
as the personification of liberal, individual, and
secular thinking.

*An ethics of life in society*

The two speakers agreed to a dialogue on the
following subject: "The Pre-political Moral
Foundations of a Free State". In other words,
they were to speak about the bases of a society
worthy of men. Cardinal Ratzinger gave his text
the title: "That Which Holds the World Together". A fundamental reflection of this kind
permits us to see the basic assumptions and
axioms and ultimate religious or secular justifications of each speaker's position, since he is
inviting the other to make a critical examination
of this position. In the case of Jürgen Habermas,
this is the practical reason of a postmetaphysical,
secular thinking; in the case of Joseph Ratzinger, we have the reality, antecedent to every
rational societal decision that may be taken, of

man as a creature who receives his life from his Creator.

## *A text that challenges the reader*

I do not propose to offer an introduction to the contents of this book, far less anticipate what the speakers have to say by summarizing their lectures. But I do wish to emphasize the clear advantage that this book has, thanks to its very compact and not excessively long texts, over more detailed and voluminous dissertations on similar topics. Here, the reader can enter an intensive conversation that concentrates on the essential issues. He can examine two forms of argumentation that are congruent in themselves and that offer a justification of the positions that the speakers hold. As both Jürgen Habermas and Joseph Ratzinger underline, their arguments arrive at very similar consequences in the "operative sphere", while pointing to clear alternatives in the justification they propose for ethical conduct, in the question of the acceptance of propositions of the law, or in the "soil out of which motivation grows" (as Ratzinger puts it).

We can learn a great deal from the systematics and structure of the basic argument that each man puts forward. And at the same time, it is really exciting to hear perspectives that one had not expected from that particular speaker. This is certainly a text that deserves intellectual curiosity.

The space that opens up between the two clearly differentiated theses challenges us to formulate our own convictions and make these concrete, just as happened in the lively discussion that followed the two statements on January 19, 2004; unfortunately, we cannot present the texts of those contributions here. The impulses provided by Habermas and Ratzinger have lost none of their freshness, and it is urgent that we take them seriously.

In the eighteenth century, there was another pope called Benedict, the fourteenth to bear that name. He reigned from 1740 to 1758. As one of the leading intellectuals of his day, he exchanged many letters with Voltaire, the great proponent of the Enlightenment (and critic of the Church). Both at that time and today, the Pope and the philosopher of the Enlightenment are the prototypes of a dialogue that makes its own contribution in our time to deciding the shape of our world's future.

> Dr. Florian Schuller
> Director
> Catholic Academy in Bavaria

# Pre-political Foundations of the Democratic Constitutional State?

By Jürgen Habermas

The topic that has been proposed for our discussion reminds me of a question that Ernst Wolfgang Böckenförde summed up in the mid-1960s in the following pregnant formula: Does the free, secularized state exist on the basis of normative presuppositions that it itself cannot guarantee?[1] This question expresses a doubt about whether the democratic constitutional state can renew from its own resources the normative presuppositions of its existence; it also expresses the assumption that such a state is dependent on ethical traditions of a local nature. These may be traditions of one particular world view or of a religion, but in any case, they have a collectively binding character. In view of what Rawls has called the "fact of pluralism", this would indeed be an embarrassment to a state that was committed to neutrality in terms of its world view; but this consequence is not per se an argument against the assumption.

[1] E. W. Böckenförde, "Die Entstehung des Staates als Vorgang der Säkularisation" (1967), in *Recht, Staat, Freiheit* (Frankfurt am Main, 1991), pp. 92ff. (here: p. 112).

I should like to define this problem more precisely in two ways. Epistemologically speaking, this doubt evokes the question of whether, now that "law" is a straightforward matter of de facto legislation—and nothing else—it is still possible in any way to provide a secular justification of political rule, that is, a justification that is nonreligious or postmetaphysical (1). Even if such a legitimation be conceded, it remains doubtful, when we consider the element of human motivation, whether a society with a plurality of world views can achieve a normative stabilization—that is, something that goes beyond a mere *modus vivendi*—through the assumption of a background understanding that will at best remain on the formal level, limited to questions of procedures and principles (2). It may be possible to neutralize this doubt; but it still remains the case that liberal societal structures are dependent on the solidarity of their citizens. And if the secularization of society goes "off the rails", the sources of this solidarity may dry up altogether. This diagnosis cannot be dismissed out of hand, but we need not understand it in such a manner that it offers the educated defenders of religion an argument in support of their case (3). Instead, I shall suggest that we should understand cultural and societal secularization as a double learning process that compels both the traditions of the Enlightenment and the religious doctrines to reflect on their own respective limits (4). Finally, with regard to postsecular societies, we must ask which cognitive attitudes and normative expectations the liberal state must require its citizens—both believers and unbelievers—to put into practice in their dealings with each other (5).

## 1. *The justification of the secular constitutional state on the basis of the sources of practical reason*

Political liberalism (which I defend in the specific form of a Kantian republicanism)[2] understands itself as a nonreligious and postmetaphysical justification of the normative bases of the democratic constitutional state. This theory is in the tradition of a rational law that renounces the "strong" cosmological or salvation-historical assumptions of the classical and religious theories of the natural law. Naturally, the history of Christian theology in the Middle Ages, and especially of late Spanish Scholasticism, forms a part of the genealogy of human rights. Ultimately, however, the bases of the legitimation of a state authority with a neutral world view are derived from the profane sources of the philosophy of the seventeenth and eighteenth centuries. It was only at a much later date that theology and the Church tackled the intellectual

[2] J. Habermas, *Die Einbeziehung des Anderen* (Frankfurt am Main, 1996).

24

challenges of the revolutionary constitutional state. Nevertheless, if I have understood it correctly, the Catholic tradition, which is comfortable with the *lumen naturale*, has no problem in principle with an autonomous justification of morality and law (that is, a justification independent of the truths of revelation).

In the twentieth century, the post-Kantian justification of liberal constitutional principles was confronted, not so much with the remnants of the objective natural law (and of the material ethics of value), as with historicist and empiricist forms of criticism. In my view, "weak" suppositions about the normative contents of the communicative constitution of socio-cultural forms of life suffice to defend a non-decisionist concept of the validity of law both against the contextualism of a non-defeatist concept of reason and against legal positivism.

Our central task is to explain (*a*) why the democratic process is understood as a process of legitimate legislation; and (*b*) why, in the process of drawing up constitutions, democracy and human rights are interconnected from the very outset.

The explanation consists in the demonstration that (*a*), to the extent that the democratic process satisfies the conditions for an inclusive and discursive formation of opinion and will, it establishes an assumption that the results will be rationally acceptable; and that (*b*) the legal institutionalization of this kind of process of democratic legislation demands that the basic liberal and political rights be granted simultaneously.[3]

The point of reference of this strategy of justification is the constitution that the associated citizens give themselves, not the domestication of an already existing state authority. Such an authority must first be generated by the act of drawing up a democratic constitution. A "constituted" (not merely a constitutionally tamed) state authority is governed in its innermost core by the rule of law, so that political power is totally permeated by the law. The positivism with regard to the will of the state, with its roots in the German empire, that dominated German political theories from Laband and Jellinek to Carl Schmitt still left a loophole for an ethical

[3] J. Habermas, *Faktizität und Geltung* (Frankfurt am Main, 1992), chap. 3.

substance of "the state" or "the political sphere" that was not dominated by the law. But in the constitutional state, there is no ruling authority derived from something antecedent to the law.[4] Before the age of constitutions, the *prince* was completely sovereign; but the transition has left no gap that an equally sovereign *people* would need to fill, in the form of the ethos of a more or less homogeneous people.

In the light of this problematical inheritance, Böckenförde's question has been understood to mean that a completely positivistic constitutional system requires religion, or some other "sustaining force", as the cognitive guarantee of the foundations of its validity. On this view, the claim of positive law to validity would need to be based on those pre-political ethical convictions of religious or national communities. However, this conclusion is drawn only because the scholars in question overlook the point that systems of law can be legitimated only in a self-referential manner, that is, on the basis of legal procedures born of democratic procedures.

[4] H. Brunkhorst, "Der lange Schatten des Staatswillens-positivismus", *Leviathan* 31 (2003): 362–81.

Hans Kelsen and Niklas Luhmann understand these democratic procedures in a positivistic manner. But if one sees them as a method whereby legitimacy is generated by legality, there is no "deficit of validity" that would need to be filled by the ethical dimension.

The proceduralist understanding of the constitutional state, inspired by Kant, insists (against the Hegelian view of the law) that the basic principles of the constitution have an autonomous justification and that all the citizens can rationally accept the claim this justification makes.

2. *How is the solidarity of the citizens of the state reproduced?*

In what follows, I assume that the constitution of the liberal state can satisfy its own need for legitimacy in a self-sufficient manner, that is, on the basis of the cognitive elements of a stock of arguments that are independent of religious and metaphysical traditions. Even under these presuppositions, however, a doubt remains with regard to the question of motivation. When we bear in mind the role played by citizens who understand themselves to be the authors of the law, we see that the normative presuppositions for the existence of a democratic constitutional state make higher demands than would be the case if they were merely citizens of the society and "addressees" of the law. All that is expected of those addressed by the law is that they do not transgress the boundaries of the law when they exercise their subjective freedoms (and claims). The obedience due to coercive laws concerning people's freedom is one thing; the motivations and attitudes expected of citizens in their role as democratic (co-)legislators are something else.

Such citizens are expected to make active use of their rights to communication and to participation, not only in what they rightly take to be their own interests, but also with an orientation to the common good. This demands a more costly commitment and motivation, and these cannot simply be imposed by law. For example, in a democratic constitutional state, a legal obligation to vote would be just as alien as a legal requirement to display solidarity. All one can do is suggest to the citizens of a liberal society that they should be willing to get involved on behalf of fellow citizens whom they do not know and who remain anonymous to them and that they should accept sacrifices that promote common interests. This is why political virtues, even if they are only "levied" in small coins, so to speak, are essential if a democracy is to exist. They are the fruit of a socialization in which one becomes accustomed to the practices and modes of thought of a free political culture. The status of citizen is, as it were, embedded in a civil society that is nourished by springs that well forth spontaneously—springs that one may term "pre-political".

This does not mean that the liberal state is incapable of reproducing its own motivational presuppositions on the basis of its own secular elements. Doubtless, citizens are in fact motivated by ethical programs of living and by cultural ways of life to take part in the political processes whereby an opinion and a common will are formed; but we must not forget that democratic practices also develop a political dynamic of their own. It is only an undemocratic constitutional state—something we experienced long enough in Germany—that would suggest a negative reply to Böckenförde's question: "To what extent can peoples united in states live exclusively on the basis of the guarantee of the freedom of the individual *without* a uniting bond that is antecedent to this freedom?" [5] This is because the democratically composed constitutional state guarantees not only negative freedoms for the citizens of the society, who are concerned about their

[5] Böckenförde, "Entstehung des Staates", p. III.

own well-being: by granting the freedom of communication, such a state also mobilizes the participation of its citizens in the public debate about topics that concern everyone. The "uniting bond" that Böckenförde seeks is the democratic process itself—a communicative praxis that can be exercised only in common and that has as its ultimate theme the correct understanding of the constitution.

Accordingly, today's debates about the reform of the welfare state, the politics of immigration, the war in Iraq, or the abolition of compulsory military service always involve more than these individual policies: the dispute also revolves around the interpretation of constitutional principles and implicitly asks how we are to understand ourselves as citizens of the Federal Republic of Germany and as Europeans, given the plurality of our cultural ways of life, our world views, and our religious convictions. It is indeed true, if we look back over history, that a common religious background and a common language, and above all the newly awakened national consciousness, helped create a highly abstract solidarity on the part of the citizens. In the meantime, however, the republican attitudes have become detached to a large extent from this pre-political anchoring—the fact that we are not willing to die "for the Treaty of Nice" is no longer an objection to a common European constitution. Think of the political and ethical discussions about the Holocaust and the immense crimes that were committed in the name of our own government: they have made the citizens of the Federal Republic of Germany conscious of the fact that their constitution was a positive gain. This example of a self-critical "politics of memory"—which is no longer something exceptional, but is found in many other countries, too—shows how a shared patriotism linked to the constitution can be formed and can renew itself even in the political sphere.

Despite a very common misunderstanding, "patriotism linked to the constitution" means that the citizens wholeheartedly accept the principles of the constitution, not only in their abstract substance, but very specifically out of the historical context of the history of each nation. The cognitive process on its own does not suffice, if the moral substance of basic rights is to conquer people's attitudes. Taken by themselves, moral insights and the worldwide consensus in moral indignation at massive breaches of human rights would suffice only for the wafer-thin integration of the citizens of a politically structured world society (if that were ever to become a reality). An abstract solidarity, mediated by the law, arises among citizens only when the principles of justice have penetrated more deeply into the complex of ethical orientations in a given culture.

## 3. *When the societal bond breaks . . .*

Up to this point, our reflections have shown that the secular nature of the democratic constitutional state displays no internal weakness inherent in the political system as such that would pose a cognitive or motivational threat to the process of self-stabilization. This does not, however, exclude external threats. If the modernization of society as a whole went off the rails, it could well slacken the democratic bond and exhaust the kind of solidarity that the democratic state needs but cannot impose by law. This would lead to precisely the constellation envisaged by Böckenförde: namely, the transformation of the citizens of prosperous and peaceful liberal societies into isolated monads acting on the basis of their own self-interest, persons who used their subjective rights only as weapons against each other. We can also see evidence of a crumbling of citizens' solidarity in the larger context, where there is no political control over the dynamic of the global economy and the global society.

Markets, which cannot be democratized like the administration of a state, are taking over an increasing number of regulatory functions in areas of life that hitherto were held together in a normative manner, that is, by political structures or via pre-political forms of communication. This means not only that private spheres increasingly adopt an orientation to trade mechanisms that aim at profit and at the realization of individual preferences; at the same time, the sphere where public legitimation is necessary is likewise shrinking. The reduction of the citizen's field of action to the private realm is intensified by the discouraging processes whereby the democratic formation of a common opinion and will loses its functional relevance. Sometimes, this functions only to a mediocre extent in the national arenas. And this in turn means that it cannot even begin to function in those processes of decision making which are transposed onto the supranational level. The dwindling of any genuine hope that the global community would be a creative political force encourages the tendency to depoliticize the citizens. In view of the conflicts and the outrageous social injustices of a global community that is profoundly fragmented, disappointment grows with each new failure along the path (first begun in 1945) to give international law the quality of a constitution.

Postmodern theories understand these crises in a manner critical of reason, that is, not as the consequence of a selective exhaustion of the rational potential that was born in the West in the modern period, but as the logical outcome of the program of a self-destructive intellectual and societal rationalization. A radical skepticism vis-à-vis reason is profoundly alien to the Catholic tradition; but until the 1960s, Catholicism had great difficulties in understanding the secular thinking of humanism, the Enlightenment, and political liberalism. And this is why, even today, there is a ready audience for the theory that the remorseful modern age can find its way out of the blind alley only by means of the religious orientation to a transcendent point of reference. In Teheran, a colleague once said to me that the comparative study of cultures and religious sociology surely suggested that *European secularization* was the odd one out among the various developments—and that it ought to be corrected. This reminds one of the mood in the Weimar Republic in Germany after the First World War—it evokes Carl Schmitt, Martin Heidegger, or Leo Strauss.

I myself think it better not to push too far the question whether an ambivalent modern age will stabilize itself exclusively on the basis of the secular forces of a communicative reason. Rather, let us treat this undramatically, as an open, empirical question. In other words, I do not wish to speak of the phenomenon of the continued existence of religion in a largely secularized environment simply as a societal fact: philosophy must take this phenomenon seriously from within, so to speak, as a cognitive challenge. But before I follow this path in the course of our discussion, let me at least mention briefly one obvious potential sidetracking of the dialogue in another direction. Thanks to the tendency to radicalize the critique of reason, philosophy, too, has been led to a self-reflection with regard to its own religious-metaphysical origins, and it has occasionally entered a conversation with a theology that on its side has seen a point of contact in the philosophers' attempts at a post-Hegelian self-reflection of reason.[6]

---

[6] P. Neuner and G. Wenz, eds., *Theologen des 20. Jahrhunderts* (Darmstadt, 2002).

*Excursus*

The starting point for the philosophical discourse about reason and revelation is a recurrent
idea: namely, that when reason reflects on its
deepest foundations, it discovers that it owes its
origin to something else. And it must acknowledge the fateful power of this origin, for other-
wise it will lose its orientation to reason in the
blind alley of a hybrid grasp of control over its
own self. The model here is the exercise of a
repentance that is carried out (or at least set in
motion) by one's own power, a conversion of
reason by reason—irrespective of whether the
starting point of one's reflection is the self-
consciousness of the knowing and acting subject
(as in Schleiermacher) or the historicity of
the existential self-reassurance of each individual (as in Kierkegaard) or the provocative
situation of an ethical disintegration (as in
Hegel, Feuerbach, and Marx). Without initially
having any theological intention, the reason that
becomes aware of its limitations thus transcends

itself in the direction of something else. This can take the form of the mystical fusion with a consciousness that embraces the universe; it may be the despairing hope that a redeeming message will occur in history; or it may take the shape of a solidarity with those who are oppressed and insulted, which presses forward in order to hasten on the coming of the messianic salvation. These anonymous gods of the post-Hegelian metaphysics—the encompassing consciousness, the event from time immemorial, the nonalienated society—are an easy prey for theology. There is no difficulty in deciphering them as pseudonyms of the Trinity of the personal God who communicates his own self.

These attempts at the renewal of a philosophical theology in the aftermath of Hegel are at any rate more agreeable than the Nietzcheanism that merely borrows the Christian connotations of hearing and perceiving, devotion and the expectation of grace, arrival and event, in order to go behind Christ and Socrates and project into some indeterminate archaic period a thinking from which all propositions have been gouged out.—But a philosophy that is aware of its fallibility and of its fragile position within the differentiated structures of modern society will insist on the generic distinction (which is not at all meant in a pejorative sense) between the secular discourse that claims to be accessible to all men and the religious discourse that is dependent upon the truths of revelation. It differs from Kant and Hegel in that this act of drawing the grammatical borders does not make a philosophical claim to determine what (apart from that knowledge of the world which is institutionalized in human society) may be true or false in the contents of religious traditions. The respect that accompanies this refusal to utter a cognitive judgment is based on the respect due to persons and ways of life that obviously derive their integrity and authenticity from religious convictions. But more is involved here than respect: philosophy has good reasons to be willing to learn from religious traditions.

## 4. *Secularization as a twofold and complementary learning process*

On the one hand, we have the ethical abstinence of a postmetaphysical thinking, to which every universally obligatory concept of a good and exemplary life is foreign. On the other hand, we find in sacred scriptures and religious traditions intuitions about error and redemption, about the salvific exodus from a life that is experienced as empty of salvation; these have been elaborated in a subtle manner over the course of millennia and have been kept alive through a process of interpretation. This is why something can remain intact in the communal life of the religious fellowships—provided of course they avoid dogmatism and the coercion of people's consciences—something that has been lost elsewhere and that cannot be restored by the professional knowledge of experts alone. I am referring to adequately differentiated possibilities of expression and to sensitivities with regard to lives that have gone astray, with regard to societal pathologies, with regard to the failure of individuals' plans for their lives, and with regard to the deformation and disfigurement of the lives that people share with one another. The asymmetry of the epistemological claims allows us to affirm that philosophy must be ready to learn from theology, not only for functional reasons, but also (when we recall philosophy's successful "Hegelian" learning processes) for substantial reasons.

This is because the mutual compenetration of Christianity and Greek metaphysics not only produced the intellectual form of theological dogmatics and a hellenization of Christianity (which was not in every sense a blessing). It also promoted the assimilation by philosophy of genuinely Christian ideas. This work of assimilation has left its mark in normative conceptual clusters with a heavy weight of meaning, such as responsibility, autonomy, and justification; or history and remembering, new beginning, innovation, and return; or emancipation and fulfillment; or expropriation, internalization, and embodiment, individuality and fellowship. Philosophy has indeed transformed the original religious meaning of these terms, but without emptying them through a process of deflation and exhaustion. One such translation that salvages the substance of a term is the translation of the concept of "man in the image of God" into that of the identical dignity of all men that deserves unconditional respect. This goes beyond the borders of one particular religious fellowship and makes the substance of biblical concepts accessible to a general public that also includes those who have other faiths and those who have none. Walter Benjamin was a philosopher who sometimes succeeded in making translations of this kind.

When we see how the religious shell is stripped of potentially significant concepts in a manner that promotes secularization, we can give Böckenförde's theory a harmless meaning. I have mentioned the diagnosis that affirms that the balance achieved in the modern period between the three great media of societal integration is now at risk, because the markets and the power of the bureaucracy are expelling social solidarity (that is, a coordination of action based on values, norms, and a vocabulary intended to promote mutual understanding) from more and more spheres of life. Thus it is in the interest of the constitutional state to deal carefully with all the cultural sources that nourish its citizens' consciousness of norms and their solidarity. This awareness, which has become conservative, is reflected in the phrase: "postsecular society".[7]

This refers not only to the fact that religion is holding its own in an increasingly secular environment and that society must assume that religious fellowships will continue to exist for the foreseeable future. The expression "postsecular" does more than give public recognition to religious fellowships in view of the functional contribution they make to the reproduction of motivations and attitudes that are societally desirable. The public awareness of a post-secular society also reflects a normative insight that has consequences for the political dealings of unbelieving citizens with believing citizens. In the postsecular society, there is an increasing consensus that certain phases of the "modernization

[7] K. Eder, "Europäische Säkularisierung—ein Sonderweg in die postsäkulare Gesellschaft?", *Berliner Journal für Soziologie* 3 (2002): 331–43.

of the public consciousness" involve the assimilation and the reflexive transformation of both religious and secular mentalities. If both sides agree to understand the secularization of society as a complementary learning process, then they will also have cognitive reasons to take seriously each other's contributions to controversial subjects in the public debate.

## 5. *How should believing and unbelieving citizens treat one another?*

On the one hand, the religious consciousness has been compelled to accept processes of accommodation. In its origins, every religion is a "world view" or a "comprehensive doctrine" in the sense that it claims the authority to give structure to an entire way of life. Under the conditions created by the secularization of knowledge, the neutralization of the state authorities, and the universalization of religious freedom, religion was compelled to abandon this claim to a monopoly on interpretation and to a comprehensive structuring of human life. With the functional differentiation of societal subsystems, the life of the religious fellowship also becomes separated from the social milieus in which it exists. The role of the fellowship member is differentiated from that of the citizen of society. And since the liberal state depends on a political integration of the citizens which goes beyond a mere *modus vivendi*, the differentiation

48

of these various memberships must be more than an accommodation of the religious ethos to laws imposed by the secular society in such a way that religion no longer makes any cognitive claims. Rather, the universalistic legal order and the egalitarian societal morality must be inherently connected to the fellowship ethos in such a way that the one consistently proceeds from the other. John Rawls uses the image of a module to express this "embedding": although this module of secular justice is constructed with the help of foundations that are neutral in terms of world view, it must fit the clusters of argumentation that are employed by each specific form of orthodoxy.[8]

The normative expectation of the liberal state vis-à-vis the religious fellowships accords with their own interests, since this gives these fellowships the possibility of bringing their own influence to bear on society as a whole, via the public political sphere. As the more or less liberal regulations about abortion show, the burdens that this tolerance imposes are not

[8] J. Rawls, *Politischer Liberalismus* (Frankfurt am Main, 1998), pp. 76ff.

symmetrically distributed on the shoulders of believers and unbelievers alike; but, on the other hand, the secular consciousness, too, pays its price for the privilege of the freedom not to be religious, since it is challenged to deal in a self-reflexive manner with the boundaries of the Enlightenment. The understanding of tolerance in pluralistic societies with a liberal constitution demands that in their dealings with unbelievers and those of different faiths, believers should grasp that they must reasonably expect that the dissent they encounter will go on existing; at the same time, however, a liberal political culture expects that unbelievers, too, will grasp the same point in their dealings with believers.

For the citizen who is "unmusical" in religious matters, this entails the demand—which is not in the least trivial—that he identify self-critically the relationship between faith and knowledge, on the basis of what all the world knows. This is because the expectation that there will be continuing disagreement between faith and knowledge deserves to be called "rational" only when secular knowledge, too,

grants that religious convictions have an epistemological status that is not purely and simply
irrational. And this is why, in the public political arena, naturalistic world views, which owe
their genesis to a speculative assimilation of
scientific information and are relevant to the
ethical self-understanding of the citizens,[9] do
not in the least enjoy a *prima facie* advantage
over competing world views or religious un-
derstandings.

The neutrality of the state authority on questions of world views guarantees the same ethical
freedom to every citizen. This is incompatible
with the political universalization of a secularist
world view. When secularized citizens act in
their role as citizens of the state, they must not
deny in principle that religious images of the
world have the potential to express truth. Nor
must they refuse their believing fellow citizens
the right to make contributions in a religious
language to public debates. Indeed, a liberal
political culture can expect that the secularized

[9] See, for example, W. Singer, "Keiner kann anders sein, als er
ist: Verschaltungen legen uns fest: Wir sollten aufhören, von Freiheit zu reden", *Frankfurter Allgemeine Zeitung*, January 8, 2004,
p. 33.

citizens play their part in the endeavors to trans-
late relevant contributions from the religious
language into a language that is accessible to the
public as a whole.[10]

[10] J. Habermas, *Glauben und Wissen* (Frankfurt am Main, 2001).

# That Which Holds
the World Together

## The Pre-political Moral Foundations
of a Free State

By Joseph Cardinal Ratzinger

Historical developments are moving more and more quickly in today's world, and I believe that two factors in particular typify this acceleration of a process that began only slowly in the past. *First*, we have the formation of a global community in which the individual political, economic, and cultural powers become increasingly dependent on one another, touching and intersecting each other in their various existential spheres. *Secondly*, we have the development of human possibilities, of the power to make and to destroy, that poses the question of legal and ethical controls on power in a way that goes far beyond anything to which we have yet been accustomed. This lends great urgency to the question of how cultures that encounter one another can find ethical bases to guide their relationship along the right path, thus permitting them to build up a common structure that tames power and imposes a legally responsible order on the exercise of power.

The fact that Hans Küng's proposal of a "world ethos" interests so many people shows at any rate that this question has in fact been posed; and this remains a valid point, even if one agrees with Robert Spaemann's acute critique of this project.[1] This is because we must add a third factor to the two mentioned above. In the process of encounter and mutual penetration of cultures, ethical certainties that had hitherto provided solid foundations have largely disintegrated. The question of what the good is (especially in the given context of our world) and of why one must do the good even when this entails harm to one's own self—this fundamental question goes generally unanswered.

It seems to me obvious that science as such cannot give birth to such an ethos. In other words, a renewed ethical consciousness does not come about as the product of academic debates. On the other hand, it is equally indisputable that the fundamental transformation of the understanding of the world and of man that has come about thanks to the growth in scientific knowledge has played a major role in the collapse of the old moral certainties. And this means that

---

[1] R. Spaemann, "Weltethos als 'Projekt'", *Merkur*, no. 570/571:893–904.

science does have a responsibility vis-à-vis man *qua* man. In particular, it is the responsibility of philosophy to accompany critically the development of the individual academic disciplines, shedding a critical light on premature conclusions and apparent "certainties" about what man is, whence he comes, and what the goal of his existence is. To make the same point in different words: philosophy must sift the non-scientific element out of the scientific results with which it is often entangled, thus keeping open our awareness of the totality and of the broader dimensions of the reality of human existence— for science can never show us more than partial aspects of this existence.

## 1. *Power and law*

It is the specific task of politics to apply the criterion of the law to power, thereby structuring the use of power in a meaningful manner. It is not the law of the stronger, but the strength of the law that must hold sway. Power as structured by law, and at the service of the law, is the antithesis of violence, which is a lawless power that opposes the law. This is why it is important for every society to overcome any suspicion that is cast on the law and its regulations, for it is only in this way that arbitrariness can be excluded and freedom can be experienced as a freedom shared in common with others. Freedom without law is anarchy and, hence, the destruction of freedom. Suspicion of the law, revolt against the law, will always arise when law itself appears to be, no longer the expression of a justice that is at the service of all, but rather the product of arbitrariness and legislative arrogance on the part of those who have the power for it.

This is why the task of applying the criterion

of the law to power leads to a further question: How does law come into being, and what must be the characteristics of law if it is to be the vehicle of justice rather than the privilege of those who have the power to make the law? It is, on the one hand, the question of the genesis of the law, but, on the other hand, the question of its own inherent criteria. The problem that law must be, not the instrument of the power of a few, but the expression of the common interest of all, seems—at first sight—to have been resolved through the instruments whereby a democratic will is formed in society, since all collaborate in the genesis of the law. This means that it is everyone's law; it can and must be respected, precisely because it is everyone's law. And as a sheer matter of fact, the guarantee of a shared collaboration in the elaboration of the law and in the just administration of power is the basic argument that speaks in favor of democracy as the most appropriate form of political order.

And yet it seems to me that one question remains unanswered. Since total consensus among men is very hard to achieve, the process of forming a democratic will relies necessarily either on an act of delegation or else on a majority decision; depending on the importance of the question at issue, the proportion of the majority that is required may differ. But majorities, too, can be blind or unjust, as history teaches us very plainly. When a majority (even if it is an utterly preponderant majority) oppresses a religious or a racial minority by means of unjust laws, can we still speak in this instance of justice or, indeed, of law? In other words, the majority principle always leaves open the question of the ethical foundations of the law. This is the question of whether there is something that can never become law but always remains injustice; or, to reverse this formulation, whether there is something that is of its very nature inalienably law, something that is antecedent to every majority decision and must be respected by all such decisions.

The modern period has formulated a number of such normative elements in the various declarations of human rights and has withdrawn these from subjection to the vagaries of majorities. It is of course possible for the contemporary consciousness to be content with the inherent obviousness of these values. But even such a self-limitation of the act of questioning has a philosophical character! There are then, let us say, self-subsistent values that flow from the essence of what it is to be a man, and are therefore inviolable: no other man can infringe them. We will have to return later to the question of the extent to which this idea can be sustained, above all because the obviousness of these values is by no means acknowledged in every culture. Islam has defined its own catalogue of human rights, which differs from the Western catalogue. And if my information is correct, although it is true that today's China is defined by a cultural form, namely Marxism, that arose in the West, it is asking whether "human rights" are merely a typically Western invention—and one that must be looked at critically.

## 2. *New forms of power and new questions about how these are to be mastered*

When we are speaking of the relationship between power and law and about the sources of law, we must also look more closely at the phenomenon of power itself. I do not propose to try to define the essence of "power" as such. Instead, I should like to sketch the challenges that emerge from the new forms of power that have developed in the last fifty years.

The first phase of the period after the Second World War was dominated by fear of the new destructive power that the invention of the atomic bomb had placed in the hands of men. Man suddenly realized that he was capable of destroying both himself and his planet. This prompted the question: What political mechanisms are necessary in order to prevent this destruction? How can such mechanisms be discovered and made effective? How can we mobilize the ethical energies that give birth to political forms of this kind and make them work? Then, for a long period, it was the competition between the opposing power blocs, and the fear that the destruction of the other side would lead to one's own destruction, that preserved us de facto from the terrors of a nuclear war. The mutual limitation of power and the fear for one's own survival proved powerful enough to save the world.

By now, however, we are afraid, not so much of a large-scale war, as of the omnipresent terror that can make itself felt and can strike anywhere. We now see that mankind does not need a large-scale war in order to make the world uninhabitable. The anonymous powers of terror, which can be present anywhere, are strong enough to pursue everyone into the sphere of everyday life. And all the time, there is the specter of criminal elements gaining access to weapons of mass destruction and unleashing chaos in the world, independent of the established political structures. This has shifted the question about law and ethos. We now ask what are the sources on which *terror* draws. How can we succeed in eliminating, from within, this new sickness of mankind? It is shocking to see here that, at least in part, terror offers a moral legitimation for its actions. Bin Laden's messages portray terror as the response of the powerless and oppressed peoples to the arrogance of the mighty and as the righteous punishment for their arrogance and for their blasphemous high-handedness and cruelty. Clearly, for people in certain social and political situations, such motivations are persuasive. In part, terrorist actions are portrayed as the defense of religious tradition against the godlessness of Western society.

At this point, another question arises, to which we must return later. If one of the sources of terrorism is religious fanaticism—and this is in fact the case—*is then religion a healing and saving force? Or is it not rather an archaic and dangerous force* that builds up false universalisms, thereby leading to intolerance and acts of terrorism? Must not religion, therefore, be placed under the guardianship of reason, and its boundaries carefully marked off? This, of course, prompts yet another question: Who can do this? And how does one do it? But the general question remains: Ought we to consider the gradual abolishment of religion, the overcoming of religion, to be necessary progress on the part of mankind, so that it may find the path to freedom and to universal tolerance? Or is this view mistaken?

In the meantime, yet another form of power has taken center stage. At first glance, it appears to be wholly beneficial and entirely praiseworthy. In reality, however, it can become a new kind of threat to man. Man is now capable of making human beings, of producing them in test tubes (so to speak). Man becomes a product, and this entails a total alteration of man's relationship to his own self. He is no longer a gift of nature or of the Creator God; he is his own product. Man has descended into the very wellsprings of power, to the sources of his own existence. The temptation to construct the "right" man at long last, the temptation to experiment with human beings, the temptation to see them as rubbish to be discarded—all this is no mere fantasy of moralists opposed to "progress".

If we have noted the urgent question of whether religion is truly a positive force, so we must now *doubt the reliability of reason*. For in the last analysis, even the atomic bomb is a product of reason; in the last analysis, the breeding and selection of human beings is something thought up by reason. Does this then mean that it is reason that ought to be placed under guardianship? But by whom or by what? Or should perhaps religion and reason restrict each other and remind each other where their limits are, thereby encouraging a positive path? Once again, we are confronted with the question how—in a global society with its mechanisms of power and its uncontrolled forces and its varying views of what constitutes law and morality—an effective ethical conviction can be found with sufficient motivation and vigor to answer the challenges I have outlined here and to help us meet these tests.

## 3. *Presuppositions of the law:*
   *Law—nature—reason*

Our first step is to look at historical situations comparable to our own, insofar as there is anything genuinely comparable. In any case, it is worth taking a very brief glance at ancient Greece, which also experienced an Enlightenment in which a divinely based law lost its obviousness, and it became necessary to look for deeper justifications of the law. This led to the idea that in the face of a positive law that can in reality be injustice, there must be a law that derives from the nature, from the very being, of man himself. And this law must be discovered, so that it can act as a corrective to the positive law.

Closer to our own times, we have the double rupture of the European consciousness that occurred at the beginning of the modern period and made necessary a new fundamental reflection on both the contents and the source of law. First, we have the exodus from the boundaries of the European world, the Christian world, that happened when America was discovered. Now, Europeans encountered peoples who did not belong to the Christian structures of faith and law, which had hitherto been the source of law for everyone and which had given this structure its form. There was no legal fellowship with these peoples. But did this mean that they were outside the law, as some asserted at that time (and as was frequently the case in practice)? Or is there a law that transcends all legal systems, a law that is binding on men *qua* men in their mutual relationships and that tells them what to do? In this situation, Francisco de Vitoria developed the already-existing idea of the *ius gentium*, the "law of the nations"; the word *gentes* also carries the association of "pagans", "non-Christians". This designates that law which is antecedent to the Christian legal form and is charged with ordering the right relations among all peoples.

The second rupture in the Christian world took place within Christianity itself through the division in faith that led to the disintegration of the one fellowship of Christians into a number of distinct fellowships, some of which were directly hostile to each other. Once again, it was necessary to elaborate a law, or at least a legal minimum, antecedent to dogma; the sources of this law then had to lie, no longer in faith, but in nature and in human reason. Hugo Grotius, Samuel von Pufendorf, and others developed the idea of the natural law, which transcends the confessional borders of faith by establishing reason as the instrument whereby law can be posited in common.

The natural law has remained (especially in the Catholic Church) the key issue in dialogues with the secular society and with other communities of faith in order to appeal to the reason we share in common and to seek the basis for a consensus about the ethical principles of law in a secular, pluralistic society. Unfortunately, this instrument has become blunt. Accordingly, I do not intend to appeal to it for support in this conversation. The idea of the natural law presupposed a concept of nature in which nature and reason overlap, since nature itself is rational. With the victory of the theory of evolution, this view of nature has capsized:

nowadays, we think that nature as such is not rational, even if there is rational behavior in nature. This is the diagnosis that is presented to us, and there seem to be few voices today that are raised to contradict it.[2] This means that, of the various dimensions of the concept of nature on which the earlier concept of the natural law was based, only one remains. Ulpian summed this up in the early third century after Christ in the well known words: "Ius naturae est, quod natura omnia animalia docet."[3] But this is not an adequate answer to

[2] This philosophy of evolution, which still remains dominant despite corrections on individual points, is most consistently and impressively expressed by J. Monod, *Chance and Necessity: An Essay on the Natural Philosophy of Modern Biology* (New York, 1971). On the distinction between the de facto results of the investigations of the natural sciences and the philosophy that accompanies these, R. Junker and S. Scherer, eds., *Evolution: Ein kritisches Lehrbuch*, 4th ed. (Giessen, 1998), is helpful. On the debate with the philosophy that accompanies the theory of evolution, see my *Glaube—Wahrheit—Toleranz* (Freiburg im Breisgau, 2003), pp. 131–47 (English trans.: *Truth and Tolerance: Christianity and World Religions* [San Francisco, 2004]).

[3] "The law of nature is that which nature teaches all sentient beings." —On the three dimensions of the mediaeval natural law (the dynamism of Being as a whole; the orientation of that nature which is common to men and animals [Ulpian]; and the specific orientation of the rational nature of man), see the information in the article by P. Delhaye, "Naturrecht", in *Lexikon für Theologie*

our question, since we are interested, not in that which concerns all the *animalia*, but in those specifically human tasks that the reason of man has created and that cannot be resolved without the reason.

One final element of the natural law that claimed (at least in the modern period) that it was ultimately a rational law has remained, namely, *human rights*. These are incomprehensible without the presupposition that man *qua* man, thanks simply to his membership in the species "man", is the subject of rights and that his being bears within itself values and norms that must be discovered—but not invented. Today, we ought perhaps to amplify the doctrine of human rights with a doctrine of human obligations and of human limitations. This could help

---

*und Kirche*, 2nd ed., vol. 7, cols. 821–25. The concept of natural law found at the beginning of the *Decretum Gratiani* is noteworthy: "Humanum genus duobus regitur, naturali videlicet iure, et moribus. Ius naturale est, quod in lege et Evangelio continetur, quo quisque iubetur, alii facere, quod sibi vult fieri, et prohibetur, alii inferre, quod sibi nolit fieri" (The human race is governed by two things, namely, the natural law and customs. The natural law is that which is contained in the law and in the gospel, whereby each one is commanded to do to another what he wishes to be done to himself and is forbidden to inflict on another what he does not wish to be done to himself).

us to grasp anew the relevance of the question of whether there might exist a rationality of nature and, hence, a rational law for man and for his existence in the world. And this dialogue would necessarily be intercultural today, both in its structure and in its interpretation. For Christians, this dialogue would speak of the creation and the Creator. In the Indian world, this would correspond to the concept of "dharma", the inner law that regulates all Being; in the Chinese tradition, it would correspond to the idea of the structures ordained by heaven.

## 4. *The intercultural dimension and its consequences*

Before I attempt to draw conclusions, I should like to widen the perspective I have indicated up to this point. If we are to discuss the basic questions of human existence today, the intercultural dimension seems to me absolutely essential—for such a discussion cannot be carried on exclusively either within the Christian realm or within the Western rational tradition. Both of these regard themselves as universal, and they may perhaps be universal *de iure*. De facto, however, they are obliged to acknowledge that they are accepted only by parts of mankind, and that they are comprehensible only in parts of mankind—although the number of competitors is of course much smaller than an initial glance might suggest.

The most important point in this context is that there no longer exists any uniformity within the individual cultural spheres, since they are all marked by profound tensions within their

73

own cultural tradition. This is very obvious in the West. Although the secular culture is largely dominated by the strict rationality of which Jürgen Habermas has given us an impressive picture, a rationality that understands itself to be the element that binds people together, the Christian understanding of reality continues to be a powerful force. The closeness and the tension between these two poles varies: sometimes they are willing to learn from each other, but sometimes they reject each other to a greater or lesser degree.

The Islamic cultural sphere, too, is marked by similar tensions. There is a broad spectrum between the fanatical absolutism of a Bin Laden and attitudes that are open to a tolerant rationality. The third great cultural sphere, that of India—or, more precisely, the cultural spheres of Hinduism and Buddhism—is likewise marked by similar tensions, although these take a less dramatic form (at least to our eyes). These cultures, too, experience the confrontation with the claims of Western rationality and the questions posed by the Christian faith, since both Western rationality and the Christian faith are present there; they assimilate one or the other in various ways, while still trying to preserve their own identity. We can round off the picture by mentioning the tribal cultures of Africa and the tribal cultures of Latin America that have been summoned to new life by various Christian theologies of liberation. In many ways, these seem to call Western rationality into question; and this means that they also call into question the universal claim of Christian revelation.

What are the consequences of all this? The first point, I believe, is that although the two great cultures of the West, that is, the culture of the Christian faith and that of secular rationality, are an important contributory factor (each in its own way) throughout the world and in all cultures, nevertheless they are de facto not universal. This means that the question put by Jürgen Habermas' colleague in Teheran seems to me not devoid of significance—namely, the question of whether a comparative study of cultures and the sociology of religion suggest that European secularization is an exceptional development and one that needs to be corrected. I would not necessarily reduce this question to the mood of Carl Schmitt, Martin Heidegger, and Levi Strauss, that is, to a situation in which Europeans have grown weary of rationality.

At any rate, it is a fact that our secular rationality may seem very obvious to our reason, which has been formed in the West; but *qua* rationality, it comes up against its limitations when it attempts to demonstrate itself. The proof for it is in reality linked to specific cultural contexts, and it must acknowledge that it cannot as such be reproduced in the whole of mankind. This also means that it cannot be completely operative in the whole of mankind. In other words, the rational or ethical or religious formula that would embrace the whole world and unite all persons does not exist; or, at least, it is unattainable at the present moment. This is why the so-called "world ethos" remains an abstraction.

## 5. Conclusions

What, then, ought we to do? With regard to the practical consequences, I am in broad agreement with Jürgen Habermas' remarks about a postsecular society, about the willingness to learn from each other, and about self-limitation on both sides. At the end of my lecture, I should like to summarize my own view in two theses.

1. We have seen that there exist *pathologies in religion* that are extremely dangerous and that make it necessary to see the divine light of reason as a "controlling organ". Religion must continually allow itself to be purified and structured by reason; and this was the view of the Church Fathers, too.[4] However, we have also seen in the course of our reflections that there are also *pathologies of reason*, although mankind in general is not as conscious of this fact today.

[4] I have attempted to set this out in greater detail in my book *Glaube—Wahrheit—Toleranz* (see n. 2 above). See also M. Fiedrowicz, *Apologie im frühen Christentum*, 2nd ed. (Paderborn, 2001).

There is a hubris of reason that is no less dangerous. Indeed, bearing in mind its potential effects, it poses an even greater threat—it suffices here to think of the atomic bomb or of man as a "product". This is why reason, too, must be warned to keep within its proper limits, and it must learn a willingness to listen to the great religious traditions of mankind. If it cuts itself completely adrift and rejects this willingness to learn, this relatedness, reason becomes destructive.

Kurt Hübner has recently formulated a similar demand. He writes that such a thesis does not entail a "return to faith"; rather, it means "that we free ourselves from the blindness typical of our age, that is, the idea that faith has nothing more to say to contemporary man because it contradicts his humanistic idea of reason, Enlightenment, and freedom".[5] Accordingly, I would speak of a necessary relatedness between reason and faith and between reason and religion, which are called to purify and help one another. They need each other, and they must acknowledge this mutual need.

[5] K. Hübner, *Das Christentum im Wettstreit der Religionen* (Tübingen, 2003), p. 148.

2. This basic principle must take on concrete form in practice in the intercultural context of the present day. There can be no doubt that the two main partners in this mutual relatedness are the Christian faith and Western secular rationality; one can and must affirm this, without thereby succumbing to a false Eurocentrism. These two determine the situation of the world to an extent not matched by another cultural force; but this does not mean that one could dismiss the other cultures as a kind of *quantité négligeable.* For a western hubris of that kind, there would be a high price to pay—and, indeed, we are already paying a part of it. It is important that both great components of the Western culture learn to *listen* and to accept a genuine relatedness to these other cultures, too. It is important to include the other cultures in the attempt at a polyphonic relatedness, in which they themselves are receptive to the essential complementarity of reason and faith, so that a universal process of purifications (in the plural!) can proceed. Ultimately, the essential values and norms that are in some way known or sensed by all men will take on a new

brightness in such a process, so that that which holds the world together can once again become an effective force in mankind.

*Joseph Cardinal Ratzinger*
*(Pope Benedict XVI)*

Joseph Ratzinger was born on April 16, 1927, in Marktl am Inn and studied philosophy and theology in Munich and Freising, where he was ordained to the priesthood on June 29, 1951. He wrote his professorial dissertation (the *Habilitationsschrift*) on Saint Bonaventure in the Department of Fundamental Theology at the University of Munich in 1957. In the following years, he was Professor of Dogmatics and Fundamental Theology at the Philosophical and Theological Academy in Freising and, then, Professor of Fundamental Theology at the University of Bonn. From 1962 to 1965, he was the official adviser (*peritus*) of Joseph Cardinal Frings at the Second Vatican Council. He became Professor of Dogmatics and the History of Dogma at the University of Münster in 1963. He moved to a professorship at the University of Tübingen in 1966. From 1969 to 1977, he was a professor at the University of Regensburg, and became the vice president of the university in 1976.

On March 25, 1977, Joseph Ratzinger was appointed Archbishop of Munich and Freising and was created cardinal in the same year. In 1981, Pope John Paul II called him to Rome as Prefect of the Congregation for the Doctrine of the Faith and as President of the Pontifical Biblical Commission and of the International Theological Commission. From 1986 to 1992, the Cardinal headed the papal commission that drew up the *Catechism of the Catholic Church*. In 1998, Joseph Ratzinger was elected Vice-Dean and in 2002 Dean of the College of Cardinals. He has received many honors. He was a member of the Second Section of the Vatican Secretariat of State and of the Congregations for the Oriental Churches, Divine Worship and the Discipline of the Sacraments, the Bishops, the Evangelization of Peoples, and Catholic Education. In 2000, Pope John Paul II appointed him an honorary member of the Pontifical Academy of Sciences.

On April 19, 2005, Joseph Cardinal Ratzinger was elected to succeed Pope John Paul II and took the name Benedict XVI.

## Jürgen Habermas

The philosopher and sociologist Jürgen Habermas was born in Düsseldorf on June 18, 1929. He studied in Göttingen, Zurich, and Bonn and took his doctorate in 1954 with a dissertation on "The Absolute in History: On the Contradiction in Schelling's Thinking". In 1961, he wrote his professorial dissertation (the *Habilitationsschrift*) under Wolfgang Abendroth in Marburg: *Strukturwandel der Öffentlichkeit* (English translation: *The Structural Transformation of the Public Sphere* [Massachusetts Institute of Technology, 1991]). He then became Professor of Philosophy at the University of Heidelberg, where he taught until 1964. From 1964 to 1971, he was Professor of Philosophy and Sociology at the Johann Wolfgang Goethe University in Frankfurt am Main. In 1971, he moved to Starnberg, near Munich, where he and Carl Friedrich von Weizsäcker headed the Max Planck Institute for Research into Living Conditions in the Scientific-Technological World. In 1981, Habermas published his principal work, *Theorie des kommunikativen Handelns* (English translation: *The Theory of Communicative Action* [Boston, 1985]), in which he develops the concept of a "discourse free of domination". In 1983, he returned to Frankfurt am Main, where he was Professor of Philosophy until his retirement in 1994. In this period, his work concentrated on the philosophy of society and of history. His numerous honors include the Geschwister Scholl Prize (1985); the Karl Jaspers Prize (1995); the Theodor Heuss Prize (1999); and the Peace Prize of the German Bookselling Trade (2001). In 2004, he received the Kyoto Prize for his lifetime achievement. This is one of the highest honors bestowed for cultural and academic activity.

*Florian Schuller*

Msgr. Florian Schuller was born on December 9, 1946, in Augsburg, and studied philosophy and theology from 1966 to 1974 at the Pontifical Gregorian University in Rome, where he took his doctorate in 1983 under Zoltan Alszeghy with a dissertation on "The Grace of Responsibility: The Value and the Problematic Elements

84

of the Theology of Fritz Buri". In 1973, Julius Cardinal Döpfner ordained him to the priesthood in Rome. He was then Prefect in the German-Hungarian College in Rome and returned to pastoral work in Germany in 1974. In 1983, he was appointed parish priest of the University and Technical College in Augsburg. From 1999 to 2000, he was spiritual rector of the Cusanuswerk, the organ of the episcopal conference that promotes studies. In September 2000, he was appointed director of the Catholic Academy of Bavaria in Munich.